Alex Cole

The implications of consumer behavior for marketing A case study of social class at Sainsbury

Anchor Compact

Cole, Alex: The implications of consumer behavior for marketing A case study of social class at Sainsbury. Hamburg, Anchor Academic Publishing 2014

Buch-ISBN: 978-3-95489-264-8
PDF-eBook-ISBN: 978-3-95489-764-3
Druck/Herstellung: Anchor Academic Publishing, Hamburg, 2014

Bibliografische Information der Deutschen Nationalbibliothek:
Die Deutsche Nationalbibliothek verzeichnet diese Publikation in der Deutschen Nationalbibliografie; detaillierte bibliografische Daten sind im Internet über http://dnb.d-nb.de abrufbar

Bibliographical Information of the German National Library:
The German National Library lists this publication in the German National Bibliography. Detailed bibliographic data can be found at: http://dnb.d-nb.de

All rights reserved. This publication may not be reproduced, stored in a retrieval system or transmitted, in any form or by any means, electronic, mechanical, photocopying, recording or otherwise, without the prior permission of the publishers.

Das Werk einschließlich aller seiner Teile ist urheberrechtlich geschützt. Jede Verwertung außerhalb der Grenzen des Urheberrechtsgesetzes ist ohne Zustimmung des Verlages unzulässig und strafbar. Dies gilt insbesondere für Vervielfältigungen, Übersetzungen, Mikroverfilmungen und die Einspeicherung und Bearbeitung in elektronischen Systemen.

Die Wiedergabe von Gebrauchsnamen, Handelsnamen, Warenbezeichnungen usw. in diesem Werk berechtigt auch ohne besondere Kennzeichnung nicht zu der Annahme, dass solche Namen im Sinne der Warenzeichen- und Markenschutz-Gesetzgebung als frei zu betrachten wären und daher von jedermann benutzt werden dürften.

Die Informationen in diesem Werk wurden mit Sorgfalt erarbeitet. Dennoch können Fehler nicht vollständig ausgeschlossen werden und die Diplomica Verlag GmbH, die Autoren oder Übersetzer übernehmen keine juristische Verantwortung oder irgendeine Haftung für evtl. verbliebene fehlerhafte Angaben und deren Folgen.

Alle Rechte vorbehalten

© Anchor Academic Publishing, ein Imprint der Diplomica® Verlag GmbH
http://www.diplom.de, Hamburg 2014
Printed in Germany

Abstract

This particular research is aimed at finding the marketing implication of influence of social class on consumer behavior for Sainsbury. Social classes differ in respect of behaviors, attitudes, and preferences. To investigate the consumer behavior and social class relationship, triangulation methodology has been adopted. A sample of 75 consumers of Sainsbury has been selected through convenience sampling. A questionnaire has been designed to collect data from sample. The findings showed that most of the respondents belonged to middle and lower social classes. The research found that middle and lower classes spend major part of their income on food and necessities of life whereas upper class spends its income on luxuries. It has been found that upper class uses internet for getting information about products and services of Sainsbury. Middle class uses televisions and newspaper for getting information about products and services of company. Upper class has more intentions of online shopping as compared to other classes. Upper classes have more attitude of investing in profitable projects. It has been found that lower and middle classes use credit cards for shopping and take bank loans for fulfilling their needs. Marketers can identify needs and preferences of different social classes from results of this particular research. Research has been limited to the findings only which have been collected from a small sample.

Contents

Abstract 1
Chapter One 7
Introduction 7
1.1   Background 7
   1.1.1   Defining Consumer Behavior 7
   1.1.2   Consumer Behavior in Context of Social Class 8
1.2   Aims and Objectives of Research 8
1.3   Research Questions 9
1.4   Significance and Scope of Research 9
1.5   Research Structure 10
Chapter Two 12
Literature Review 12
2.1   Defining Consumer Behavior and Social Class 12
2.2   Social Class Measurement 12
2.3   Social Image 14
2.4   Existing Literature about Social Class and Consumer Behavior 14
2.5   Social Class and Leisure Activities 17
2.6   Living style 17
2.7   Motivation 18
2.8   Shopping Behaviors 18
2.9   Social Classes in United Kingdom 19
2.10   Summary of Chapter 21
Chapter Three 23
Methodology 23
3.0   Introduction 23
3.1   Research Philosophy 23
3.2   Research Approach 24
3.3   Research Methods 25
3.4   Research Design 25
3.5   Data Collection Techniques 26
   3.5.1   Types of Data 26
   3.5.2   Primary data collection techniques 26
      Surveys 27
      Interviews 27

		Focus Groups	28
	3.5.3	*Comparison of primary data collection tools*	28
	3.5.4	Primary and Secondary data collection tools employed in research	28
3.6		Population and Sample	29
3.7		Validity and Reliability of Research	29
3.8		Research Ethics	30
3.9		Method of Data Analysis	30
3.10		Summary of Chapter	30

Chapter Four 31
Data Findings and Presentation 31

4.1		Introduction	31
4.2		Data Findings	31
	4.2.1	General Information	31
4.3		Chapter Summary	44

Chapter Five 45
Data Interpretation and Analysis 45

5.1		Introduction	45
5.2		Analysis of findings	45
	5.2.1	Social Class Breakdown	45
	5.2.2	Consumption preference for Food and Entertainment	46
	5.2.3	Frequency of Shopping	46
	5.2.4	Preference for Buying Durables and Nondurables	47
	5.2.5	Preference for Buying Branded, Non-branded and Fashionable Products	47
	5.2.6	Attitude of Visiting Restaurants	49
	5.2.7	Leisure Activities	49
	5.2.8	Preference for Communication Media Type	50
	5.2.9	Preference for Online Shopping	51
	5.2.10	Preference for Financial Products	51
5.3		Summary of Chapter	52

Chapter Six 53
Conclusion and Recommendations 53

6.1	Introduction	53
6.2	Conclusion	53
6.3	Implications of Research	55
6.4	Limitations	56
6.5	Future Research	56

References 57
Questionnaire 60

Chapter One
Introduction

1.1 Background

In today's competitive world where organizations are looking for high profitability and market share, consumers have taken very important place. Organizations look for capturing consumers in order to get larger market share. For this purpose a number of techniques and tools have been developed by the organizations. One of such tools is Consumer behavior which has been derived from economic theory. Consumer behavior is basically the study of factors and situations that can influence buying decisions of consumers. Consumer behavior has become very important discipline of management sciences which assists in understanding of consumers' decision making.

1.1.1 Defining Consumer Behavior

The study of consumer behavior suggests that how are consumers going to spend their resources in terms of money and effort on buying products and services (Arnold, 2002). Consumer behavior discipline not only covers decision making process of consumers but a large number of other factors are also discussed in this discipline. According to Solomon (1996) defines consumer behavior as a process which studies that how individuals or groups are going to purchase, consume, and dispose of products, services, experiences, ideas over a period of time. Blech (1998) has defined consumer behavior as a process which studies the activities that are involved in searching, selecting, purchasing and disposing of goods and services in order to satisfy needs and wants of consumers. It suggests that consumer behavior studies the whole cycle which starts from purchase of products and services and ends on disposing of products and services. Consumer behavior occurs in context of individuals, groups or organizations. There are number of factors that influence consumers to take final decision regarding purchase of a particular product or service. Consumer behavior studies the influence of these factors on buying decision of consumers. Demographics, personal characteristics, economic factors, social factors, and psychological factors affect the buying decision of consumers. From all these factors social class is an important one which influences consumer behavior. Social class in a society is basically the stratification of individuals of society on the basis of social status i.e. material wealth (Sciffman and Kanuk, 2007).

1.1.2 Consumer Behavior in Context of Social Class

Social class is hierarchical in nature where some individuals are given higher status than the others. Individuals at different hierarchical stage possess different characteristics, needs and preferences. In other words consumer behavior of different social classes differs from each other. There are number of ways of dividing a society into different classes. Society can be divided into different social classes on the basis of income, occupation or material wealth. There are three basic strata in each society that divide it into upper, middle and lower classes. These classes differ from each other in their beliefs and attitudes. In each society social stratification exists based on different aspects. Some social classes have more resources as compared to others. Due to changes in income structures these social classes exhibit different patterns of spending. A particular social class cannot live alone in a society. In fact society is composite of number of social classes that influence each other to some extents. Consumption patterns of these social classes influence each other. In this way importance of studying consumer behavior with respect to social class has a great importance. In consumer behavior discipline social classes have a great importance. Companies and marketers need to study influence of social classes on consumer behavior in order to satisfy different social classes in a society. Identical offers of companies to all social classes cannot satisfy them Marketers need to adopt different attitude towards different social classes.

This particular research is going to study the marketing implications of influence of social class on consumer behavior in United Kingdom. The research is being conducted to find the influence of social class on consumer behavior in Sainsbury in United Kingdom.

1.2 Aims and Objectives of Research

This particular research is going to discuss the consumer behavior in context of social class. The aim of this particular research is as follows:

"To study the influence of social class on consumer behavior and to find its marketing implications for in Sainsbury"

Objectives of this particular study are as follows:

- To study breakdown of social classes in the United Kingdom
- To study the relationship between social class and consumer behavior from existing literature
- To investigate different factors influencing consumer behavior in different social classes
- To study the extent to which customers of different social classes behave differently in Sainsbury
- To find the implication of the findings of research for marketing of Sainsbury

1.3 Research Questions

Research questions are very important for research project because the whole research is focused on research questions. If research questions are not developed properly, accurate results cannot be achieved. It is very important to design accurate and precise research questions in order to get accurate results of research. Questions developed for this particular research are as follows:

- What is the relationship of social class and consumer behavior?
- What are the factors which influence consumer behavior of different social classes?
- How does consumer behavior differ in different social classes in Sainsbury?
- What are the marketing implications of the study for Sainsbury?

1.4 Significance and Scope of Research

This particular research is going to research to evaluate the influence of social class on consumer behavior. Consumer behavior is very important to be studied because it assists companies to understand the wants, preferences and needs of consumers. Different social classes exist in the societies which have specific behavior towards offers of companies. Companies need to understand how to satisfy these social classes. In today's competitive world, the organizations which understand the needs and wants of customers of different social classes can lead the market while the companies which do not respond to the needs and wants of different social classes are compelled to leave the market. Thus, studying consumer behavior of different social classes is very important for companies. This particular research analyses the factors influencing consumer behavior of different social classes in Sainsbury in United Kingdom. The factors analyzed in this research are significant for the Sainsbury to satisfy the needs and wants different social classes. The research is presents the marketing implications for Sainsbury for satisfying its customers.

1.5 Research Structure

This particular research is composed of six chapters. All the chapters serve a specific purpose towards the achievement of aims and objectives of research. All these chapters have been interlinked and a coherent research has been produced. Following is the brief summary of all chapters.

Chapter 1:

It presents background of the research with aims and objectives. The current scenario in which research has been created is described here. Aims and objectives of research have been presented in this particular chapter. Research questions and significance of research has also been outlined here. The summary of all chapters is also presented here.

Chapter 2:

In literature review consumer behavior has been described in the light of previous researches. Influence of social class on consumer behavior has been described in this chapter. Literature regarding consumer behavior and social class has been explored. Different social classes have been explained in this chapter. Social structure of United Kingdom has also been explained in this chapter.

Chapter 3:

This is methodology section of research. Research philosophy, methods, and research approach has been justified according to aims and objectives of research. Data collection tools, validity and reliability and research ethics have been described in this chapter.

Chapter 4:

This chapter relates to presentation of data findings. All the findings of research have presented in the form of percentages. Graphical representation of data findings is also done.

Chapter 5:

The aim of this chapter is to analyze the data findings. All the findings of data are analyzed descriptively. Detailed discussion on data findings has been conducted. Findings are related to the secondary data in order to validate them. Each question of questionnaire has been discussed in detail. Findings are analyzed descriptively.

Chapter 6:

The last chapter presents conclusion of data findings. The whole research has been concluded here. Implications of research findings for marketing and prospects of future research are also presented in this chapter.

Chapter Two
Literature Review

2.1 Defining Consumer Behavior and Social Class

Consumer behavior is the activity that involves consumers in purchasing, consuming, and disposing of products and services (Loudon, 2001). Consumer behavior can also be defined as decisions taken by consumers for buying, consuming, and disposing of products and services, experiences, ideas, and people over a specific period of time (Wayne, 2009). This suggests that consumer behavior is the sum of all activities that are involved from buying to disposing of products and services. Consumer behavior is a broad concept that involves a number of activities involving from the very first point of buying to the disposing of products.

Myers (1971) has introduced the concept of social class in the marketing literature. Social class is basically the division of individuals of society into different groups in a hierarchy having distinct characteristics. Sciffman and Kanuk (2007) have defined social class as the stratification of whole society into different groups on the basis of material wealth. This social stratification subsists in all societies that divide individuals into different groups. Social class is basically the status that is associated with the individuals of a particular class in relation to the individuals of other classes. Social stratification can be based on power, income, lifestyle, education and wealth. The differences that exist in different social classes are very important for marketers and companies. Loudon (2007) has said that social class has close relation with the consumer behavior and even a very close relation with the buying decisions of consumers of different social classes. This suggests that needs, wants, preferences, and attitudes of individuals of different social classes differ.

2.2 Social Class Measurement

Social class measurement is basically a tool to classify the society into different classes. These classes are used by the marketers to identify consumer segments for their products and services. Social classes can be determined by following measures (Loudon, 2001):

- Subjective Measurement
- Reputational Measurement
- Objective Measurement

Subjective measure classifies social classes on the basis of self perception of individuals. Reputational measure classifies social systems on the basis of perception of others. The third measure i.e. objective measure classifies social systems on the basis socioeconomic measures.

There are three basic segments of social classes. These are upper class, middle class and lower class (Arnold, 2002).

Upper Class

Upper class has access to financial and non financial resources. This class is the wealthiest of all classes. Distinctive media and distinguished products are used by the marketers to target this particular class. This class accepts customized products and services. Arnold (2002) individuals who are new in this particular class have desire to be visible in changed social class.

Middle Class

This class is composed of working people. Middle class has been emerging throughout the world (Arnold, 2002). This class focuses on education and marriage issues more as compared to others. Emotions are considerably high in this social class so marketers target this class with emotional values. Individuals of this social class have desire to progress at upper class.

Lower Class

Majority of the population of world is composed of lower class. Lower class is characterized by low income, low education, and minorities. Individuals of this class have high technical education. Lower class usually spends money on basic necessities of life e.g. food, shelter, and clothes (Arnold, 2002). Mass media is used to target lower class by the marketers.

2.3 Social Image

There are numb are of factors that affect relationship between consumer behavior and social class. One of such factors is self image associated with an individual in a particular social class (Rookes and Wilson, 2000).

The perception of self image is basically the process of recognition and interpretation of external stimuli to which individuals are exposed. According to self image perception view, individuals in one social class perceive others on the basis of their job, salary, house, and clothing. The interpretation of these social factors gives shape to the consumer behavior of individuals.

Cognitive self image is formed on the basis of their belonging to a particular ethnic group other group in a society (Pintrich, 2005). It is basically the personalization of particular state of mind that is owned by the individuals in particular society. It allows individuals to evaluate themselves.

Normative image refers to the idea by which individuals consider their view in the eyes of others and decide about the social class in which they want to be placed. This can be done either consciously or unconsciously by the individuals. Normative image of individual has relationship with the consumer behavior (Adams, 1993). Middle social class seeks for opportunities than can associate it with the upper class in order to satisfy its normative image and gain imaginary acceptance from the members of society. A single group can have different levels and forms of normative self image (Hoyer and Maccinis, 2009). Cognitive and normative image can affect the preferences and attitudes of individuals in different social classes and ultimately affect consumer behavior.

2.4 Existing Literature about Social Class and Consumer Behavior

Social class has been extensively studied with respect to consumer behavior. A number of researchers have established relationship between social class and consumer behavior. In marketing theory consumer behavior and social class have a considerable place. Mirela (2006) says that consumer behavior has close relation with the social class.

Every society has social stratification that is permanent in nature and all members of one social class have distinct characteristics. A single factor does not determine the social class but a number of factors determine social class structure. Kotler and Armstrong (2007) say that marketers need to concentrate on the factors that stratify a society because each social class has distinct characters that can affect its consumer behavior. They further said that consumers in each social class exhibit similar attitude, behavior and preferences.

Social classes are created by the groups of people having same social status (O'Doughtery, 2007). The individuals of these groups meet with each other frequently and share similar values with each other. The sense of belonging possessed by the individuals of these social classes is passed on to the consumer behavior of these classes.

Noel (2008) has found that social class motivates individuals composing it to buy particular goods and services. He found three ways by which a social class affects consumer behavior. These three ways are conspicuous consumption, status float behavior and trickledown effect.

Conspicuous consumption is basically the purchasing and consuming of costly products and services. This concept depicts the social status of an individual (Noel, 2008). The next concept is trickledown effect which refers to the idea that lower classes observe the buying behavior of upper classes and try to copy them. This behavior occurs when lower social classes are inspired by the attitudes and behavior of upper classes (Noel, 2008). The final affect is status float that refers to the idea when upper classes copy the attitude and buying behavior of lower classes. This affect is opposite to that of trickledown effect. Lower classes have very high conspicuous oriented consuming behavior which is against their social status (Loudon, 2001). This is because lower classes spend high income on expensive products like clothes and jewelry only to show off others in order to overcome their inferiority complex. Individuals of middle class spend more income in order achieve something. People in this class have been found to prefer social acceptability of products rather than their functionality. They try to buy those things which depict their high image in the society.

Social classes are characterized by varying access to financial and non financial resources. Social classes also have different choices and use of products and services. Upper class has a pool of resources and spends its sources on lavish life styles like purchase of bonds and branded wines. On the other hand lower class spends its resources on purchasing derby tick and local and cheap wine (Loudon, 2007). It is not necessary that these assumptions will always come true and apply to all members of a social class. Any individual in a social class can differ from general behavior of his or her social class (Loudon, 2007).

Different social classes have different behaviors regarding leisure time, brand preferences and consumption patterns. Keiser and Kuehl (1972) have established a relationship between social class and brand identification. Income is very important factor that has association with social classes but it becomes irrelevant when products of low social value are purchased (Schaninger, 1981).

It has been argued by the Loudon (2007) that social classes differ in the consumer behavior because of differences in their financial status and education level. The individuals of upper social classes have more opportunities for consumer learning as compared to the individuals of lower social classes. Young, (2003) has analyzed that individuals of upper social class have more choices of food as compared to those of lower class. He further argues that children of upper social class play active role in changing habits. He found that preference for food and other products of individuals of different social classes change by their interaction with the peers.

Social classes differ in their consumption behavior. Upper social classes have high resources so they have high probability of more consumption as compared to lower classes. Mirela (2006) has established a relationship between food, clothing, and financial consumption behaviors and social classes. His findings suggest that upper social class consumers more macrobiotic food as compared to lower social class. While shopping clothes lower social class considers about price to a great extent and ignores quality as compared to upper social class. Mirela (2006) has also found that higher social classes attend theaters frequently in their leisure time whereas lower classes do not have such interests because of low interest in educational activities. When the frequency of visiting restaurants was compared, it was found in his findings that lower and middle classes have less frequency of visiting restaurants as compared to that of higher social classes. When compared about housing facilities it has been found that members of upper social classes have owned apartments whereas lower social classes rely on rented homes (Mirela, 2006). It has also been found that upper social class is much conscious about decoring houses as compared to that of lower social class (Mirela, 2006).

Martineau (1958) suggested that social classes have relation with the perceived risk, choice and selection of store. Risk is perceived on the basis of resources countered to check level of risk. There are also differences in values, interpersonal attitudes, communication source selection, and shopping behaviors of individuals in different social classes (Levy, 1966). There are differences in gaining credits from banks in different social classes. Lower social classes have more intentions of buying today and paying tomorrow (Mathews and Slocum, 1969). Different social classes have different attitudes towards fashionable goods, sources of shopping information and influences from other groups of society (Rich and Jain, 1968).

2.5 Social Class and Leisure Activities

Leisure activities are those activities that are other than the usual work. It depends on the individual choice and preference that where he/she wants to spend leisure time. Individuals in different social classes have different preferences about spending leisure time. Burdge (1969) has found that different social classes differ in their leisure activities which basically depend on the social activities of individuals. Members of social classes that have different occupations and involvement in the social groups have different preferences for spending leisure time. As the involvement in occupation increases, preference of leisure activities changes (Burdge, 1969). It has been analyzed by Young (2003) that upper social classes spend their leisure time in activities which involve high expenditures such as at golf clubs or tennis fields. Individuals of each social class spend their leisure activities with their peers. He concludes that social strata differs have different leisure activities because they belong to different groups.

2.6 Living style

Living styles of individuals in different social classes vary from each other. Variation in the lifestyles of individuals is one of the reasons of changed consumer behaviors of different social classes (Solomon, 2004). Individuals are grouped into different classes on the basis of standards of employment and income levels (Solomon, 2004). Individuals in each social class have a distinct lifestyle which assists them in satisfaction of their cognitive self image. To become fit in a particular lifestyle it becomes important for individuals to possess a specific consumer behavior different from others.

2.7 Motivation

Lantos (2010) has identified motivation an influencing factor on consumer behavior. According to him it is most important psychological factor that can affect consumer behavior. Motivation refers to the question that why people adopt a particular type of consumer behavior and how does consumer behavior can be changes for the well being of society or organizations (Lantos,2010).

A number of sub factors of motivation have been recognized by Lantos (2010) that affect consumer behavior in a society directly or indirectly. The very first aspect of motivation influencing consumer behavior identified by Lantos (2010) is internal state of individuals that does not have a close relation with direct observation. The internal state of individuals is shaped by the interactions among people. Individuals in a particular social class interact with each other frequently and share certain values. This interaction of individuals in a social group influences internal state of individuals that ultimately affects consumer behavior. Motivation of individuals allows them to achieve a particular goal or objective. Until the goal or objective has not been achieved, individuals in social class remain motivated. Motivation also affects problem recognition and the process of solving problems of individuals. These two steps are critical to the buying process of individuals which is essential component of consumer behavior. Schiffman, L.G., & Kanuk (2007) have said that individuals within social classes differ in their choices regarding taste and fashion of goods. They further said that social class also determines the place where individuals shop. Individuals shop from retail stores, supermarkets, local stores or through online. Individuals prefer to go to a shopping site that is according to their social status. Their findings also suggest that social class also has relationship with the spending, savings and credit. Lower social classes tend to get credit in order to fulfill their basic needs. Middle class prefers to save money and also takes credit in order to satisfy normative cognitive image. Social classes also differ in terms of availing means of communication (Schiffman, L.G., & Kanuk, 2007).

2.8 Shopping Behaviors

Social classes differ in terms of shopping behaviors. Reasons and purpose of shopping differs in most of individuals. Some individuals shop for fulfilling their needs and some shop as an enjoyment. Lower classes enjoy acquiring new items and clothes. On the other hand upper middle class prefers to have pleasant store atmosphere with attractive display and location

(Albert and David, 1993). It has been found that upper and middle class individuals shop more frequently than those of lower class. Their findings suggest that higher social status persuades individuals to give more importance to shopping. Middle and lower classes do not give more consideration to shopping and their individuals tend to browse in the markets without buying anything. Discount stores are selected by the lower classes for shopping. On the other hand highly sophisticated and fashionable stores are selected by the individuals of upper classes. Marketers can get valuable information from consumer behavior of different social classes. Marketers can get valuable information regarding the type of products required by a particular social class (O'Doughtery, D., 2007).

Individuals of upper social class organize the shopping in a purposeful way. They want to get knowledge about what they shop (Albert and David, 1993). A proper planning is done for selecting items to be bought, place from where is to shop and about time when to shop. Prior to purchasing information is searched through various sources regarding shopping. Newspapers, internet, broachers and reports are analyzed before shopping heavy items (Albert and David, 1993).

Middle social class emphasizes more on the environment of stores. Clean, organized and attractive store environment appeals to this social class. They prefer to shop through stores in which employees know about their social status and gives importance to them (Albert and David, 1993). This social class ahs more education and knowhow of computer. Internet media is also frequently used by the upper class. These attitudes direct this social class to internet shopping. It has been found by the findings of Albert and David (1993) that upper middle and upper social classes have more tendency and intentions for online shopping than other social classes. Middle social class tends to work more during shopping. This social class displays more worry while shopping. This social class is value conscious. Because of limited resources and high desires, this class suffers from anxiety. Individuals of this class try to get value of money during shopping. To fulfill desires, they tend to do to discounts stores (Albert and David, 1993).

2.9 Social Classes in United Kingdom

Different societies have different social structures which vary from each other. In some societies lower social strata are two and in some societies this is more than two. As discussed earlier that most of the societies are divided into three main classes i.e. upper class, middle class and lower class. In an open society individuals have freedom to move across different social classes. The social structure of United Kingdom has been historically very important that is different from other countries of the world. In this way it will be interesting to study the consumer behavior across different social classes of United Kingdom. A number of changes have been occurred in the social structure of United Kingdom regarding intensity and mobility. The study of consumer behavior in social structure of United Kingdom provides a dynamic picture of changing trends consumers over a period of time.

Pantazis, Gordon and Levitas (2006) suggest that social structure of United Kingdom is composed of professionals, managers and workers. Professional and mangers hold the professions of the country whereas workers tend to work for spending time and earning money. Their findings suggest that working class gives more importance to cheap sources of entertainment because it focuses on keeping the life regular. Expensive sources of entertainment are avoided by this class. Television is given more importance by the working class. Marketers can target working class by using television as a mode of advertisement. Findings of Pantazis, Gordon and Levitas (2006) present a very interesting reality about working class that most of the individuals in this class carpet the floors of homes in order to avoid expenses for cleaning the floor. Banerjee and Batini (2003) found that one seventh of the population of United Kingdom is composed of lower class. They found that income of individuals of lower classes of United Kingdom is equal to their expenditures. It means that individuals of lower class in United Kingdom have zero saving rates. This class tends to borrow money for fulfilling needs and luxuries.

In United Kingdom social classes exist on the basis of income level of individuals (Social Research Update, 1995). This update has provided official categories of social classes in United Kingdom on income basis. The social classes identified by this update are: professional occupation holder, managerial and technical occupation holder, skilled holders including physical or non physical workers, partly skilled holders and untrained professionals. This stratification is done on the basis of employment level of individuals which results in differences in income levels. People gave been categorized into the above categories and socially they are treated on the basis of this classification in United Kingdom. Individuals having more income tend to spend more in order to consume more. This is done to get high social acceptance in order to satisfy normative self image. Expensive products are symbol of high social status so individuals who have limited resources and cannot spend more on luxuries try to relate themselves in different ways in order to gain social acceptance.

The literature discussed about the social class and consumer behavior suggests that social classes have significant relationship with the consumer behavior. Marketers and companies need to consider different attitudes, preferences and behaviors of social classes. The information about the attitudes of social classes can assist marketers to design specific products and services for specific social classes.

2.10 Summary of Chapter

Social classes are basically stratification of societies into different groups on the basis of occupation, income and material wealth. Basically a society can be divided into three main classes. These are: upper class, middle class and lower class. Upper class has pool of resources and is given high social status. Lower class has limited resources and is given low social status. Consumer behavior is basically the process through which people purchase, consume, and dispose of goods and services. This process varies across different social classes because income differences in these classes are very prominent. Literature discussed has suggested that lower social class shops less frequently because it has limited resources. Upper social classes have more frequency of shopping. Individuals in different social classes exhibit different patterns of shopping. Previous researchers have proved that lower classes tend to go towards discount stores for shopping. Upper social classes tend to shop from specialty stores. Some researchers have proved that upper social classes have more positive attitude for online shopping as compared to that of lower classes. This is because upper social class is more exposed to internet media. Three effects have been discussed in the literature regarding social classes' consumer behavior. These are conspicuous consumption, status float behavior and trickledown effect. Conspicuous affect is that when consumers buy expensive goods and services. Status float affect is that when upper social classes copy the consumer behavior of lower classes. Trickledown effect is opposite to status float in which lower classes copy the consumer behavior of upper classes in order to gain social acceptability. Literature has also discussed social class structure of United Kingdom. In

United Kingdom social classes have been defined on the basis of occupation. Professionals, managers, and workers compose social structure of United Kingdom. Findings of some previous researchers regarding consumer behavior of different social classes have been extensively discussed.

Chapter Three
Methodology

3.0 Introduction

Each research follows a particular methodology. Researchers can find different results by adopting different methodologies. It is very important for researchers to adopt a particular methodology which must be aligned with the aims and objectives of research. In this chapter research philosophy, approach, and methods have been described and justified. Data collection methods and tools have also been outlined here.

3.1 Research Philosophy

For evaluating the consumer behavior of different social classes in Sainsbury, research philosophies create background for the research. They include attitudes, assumptions and beliefs of researchers for conducting a particular research. A number of choices are available to the researcher for evaluating influence of social class on consumer behavior. It is very important for researchers to justify the adopted approach according to aims and objectives of research and also to give reasons for leaving the other philosophies (Blaikie (2000).

The first choice for studying the consumer behavior in different social classes is realism which believes that what is true in a laboratory is not always valid for the real world. It suggests that reality results from taming of different social aspects. Realists research different issues by considering their own particular viewpoint (Hatch and Cunliffe, 2006). This philosophical approach is closer towards natural sciences, so it is not selected for studying the consumer behavior of different social classes.

The second choice for studying the consumer behavior in different social classes is interpretivism which finds solutions of different problems on the basis of different beliefs and values. It works against positivists (Easterby et al., 2008). By this philosophical approach, researchers can study the consumer behavior of different social classes through multiple realities. Interpretivists study different social factors and interpret them on their own points of view.

Because of this feature of Interpretivists, consumer behavior of social classes is not studied as it would create bias results.

Consumer behavior of social class is studied through positivism. Positivists deal with the development and testing of research hypothesis. Existing theories are evaluated by positivists and hypotheses are formed for testing. Positivists reject of accept hypothesis on the basis of statistical tools (Saunders, Lewis and Thornhill, 2007). Through direct observations and experiences, consumer behavior of different social classes can be studied by positivists. By using empirical and quantitative methods such as surveys, positivism approach is used for studying the consumer behavior of customers of different social classes in Sainsbury. This philosophy is suitable for evaluating the aims and objectives of research in effective manner.

3.2   Research Approach

In order to study the consumer behavior of different social classes, there are two types of research approaches. These are deductive and inductive research approaches. In this particular study, both approaches have been incorporated.

Deductive approach deals with study of existing theories and models. The influence of social class on consumer behavior has been explored through existing researches by deductive approach of research. One of the objectives of this research is to evaluate the consumer behavior and social class linkage through existing literature. For this purpose, existing literature will be explored regarding consumer behavior and social classes. Thus, deductive approach is appropriate for evaluating the objectives of research.

The second research approach i.e. inductive approach constructs new theories and models through experiments and observations. It deals issues from specific to general viewpoint (Saunders et al., 2009). The influence of social class on consumer behavior in Sainsbury has been analyzed through inductive research approach. The specific view of the study is the consumer behavior of different social classes in Sainsbury and the general view of the study is its marketing implications. These two research approaches are important to explore the aims and objectives of research. A single research approach could not discover all the aims and objectives of research so single approach has been avoided in this particular research.

3.3 Research Methods

Researcher has two choices of research methods for this particular research. These are qualitative and quantitative research methods. Triangulation research methodology deals with both methods (Adela, 2004). Triangulation methodology is more useful and effective as compared to a single choice.

In this particular research triangulation methodology has been employed. Qualitative research methods evaluate behaviors, perceptions and attitudes of people of societies (Marshall & Rossman, 1999). In this particular research, attitudes, perceptions and behavior of different social classes are explored through qualitative approach. Existing theories are explored regarding social class and consumer behavior which is basically qualitative method of research. By using this approach, the researcher has explored consumer behavior of social classes with the help of words rather than numeric values. Through qualitative approach, the influence of social class on consumer behavior from perspective of previous researches has been discussed in the literature review. Quantitative research method deals with the development of research hypothesis on the basis of existing theories. The influence of social class on consumer behavior of Sainsbury is found with the help of quantitative research methods. Quantitative research methods involve numeric data. Although in this particular research, complicated and extensive numerical data or calculations are not involved, but there are simple calculations like percentages for studying the consumer behavior of social classes in Sainsbury.

The use of both research methods in this study has proved to be very effective. The findings of qualitative methods have complemented those of quantitative methods. In this way, consumer behavior of different social classes has been studied effectively.

3.4 Research Design

This particular research is a case study of Sainsbury. A case study research design studies particular unit e.g. a single organization or individual. Case study research design is best design for this particular research in order to study influence of social class on consumer behavior in United Kingdom because it studies the consumer behavior of different social classes in detail. This will be very helpful for determining the marketing implications of the study. Through case study research designs, questionnaire or interview technique of data collection will be employed. Data collection tools of the research are selected on the basis of research design.

3.5 Data Collection Techniques

3.5.1 Types of Data

There are two types of data i.e. primary and secondary. In this particular research, both kinds of data have been employed to study the consumer behavior of different social classes in Sainsbury. Primary data is first hand data which does not exist in the theories and literature. Researchers collect it for the first time. It is most recent and original form of data (Saunders et al., 2009). In order to study the consumer behavior of social classes in Sainsbury, it is important to incorporate primary data.

Secondary data exists in the literature in the form of theories and model. Collection of work of pervious researchers and authors forms base of secondary data. It can be manipulated by the previous researchers so biasness is high in secondary data as compared to primary data in which no manipulation has been conducted. In order to evaluate the objective of the research for exploring the existing studies on consumer behavior of social classes, secondary data has been incorporated.

Use of both types of data has been very beneficial for studying the consumer behavior of different social classes in Sainsbury. The findings of primary data have complimented findings of secondary data and an effective understanding of consumer behavior and social class has been made.

3.5.2 Primary data collection techniques

There are various tools of primary data collection which are adopted by the researchers for conducting research. Some of primary data collection tools which can be considered for studying the consumer behavior of different social classes are surveys, interviews and focus group discussions. Following is the explanation of these tools.

Surveys

Surveys technique is used to collect data from a large population in short time. It helps in determining traits and behaviors of people in short time. This approach can be cost effective and time saving for studying the consumer behavior of different social classes in Saisnbury. Usually, questionnaire is used to collect primary data through surveys. Researcher interacts with participants to limited extent. So if consumer behavior of different social classes will be studied through survey approach of data collection, there would be less biasness in the results. There can be some problems while collecting data through survey. Respondents may have problems in understanding purpose of questions of survey, because of low interaction of researcher with them. In this way there are chances of getting vague responses of participants in the data (Russ and Preskill, 2001). If primary data from a large population is to be collected, survey is the best choice. For this particular study, survey technique can be one of the valuable approaches.

Interviews

The second approach which can be considered for studying the consumer behavior of different social classes is interview. Interviews are used to collect data from participants in direct discussion with them. Qualitative data is gathered during interviews. Three types of interviews i.e. structured, unstructured, and semi structured can be conducted with the customers of Sainsbury for evaluating consumer behavior. In structured interviews, a questionnaire is developed for asking questions from respondents. No additional question is added during structured interviews. In semi structured interviews, researcher can ask additional questions other than questionnaire. In unstructured interviews researcher asks direct questions and does not use any questionnaire. Unstructured interviews allow more chances of detailed discussion from participants. Specific atmosphere is needed for conducting interviews which can be costly for collecting data for this particular research. Another disadvantage of interview is that in interviews interaction of researcher with participants is high which can create biasness in the results (Russ and Preskill, 2001). Thus, interview approach will be considered as a second priority for collecting data from respondents in order to study consumer behavior of different social classes.

Focus Groups

The third approach which can be considered for collecting data for studying consumer behavior in different social classes is focus group discussion. Focus group is composed of six to twelve people having parallel characteristics. A mediator is asked to conduct focus group discussion, who asks opinions, views and beliefs of participants regarding a particular situation. This can be very costly and time consuming approach for this particular research. Focus group discussions generate qualitative form of data. Participants are asked to say whatever comes in their mind regarding the object of discussion (Krueger and Casey, 2000). This approach will be considered as third priority for collecting data in order to study consumer behavior of different social classes in Sainsbury.

3.5.3 Comparison of primary data collection tools

Survey technique is less costly and time saving as compared to focus group discussions and interviews. In surveys there is probability of vague responses because researcher has little interaction with respondents. On the other hand, focus group discussions and interviews produce clear responses because researcher can explain the purpose of questions to respondents. Interviews and focus group discussions require proper arrangement which contribute in high cost. Primary data collected through survey technique has minimum biasness due to less interaction of researcher with respondents. On the other hand researcher interacts with respondents to high level during interviews and focus group discussions which can create biasness in data. Researchers select tool of primary data collection by leveraging pros and cons of data all collection tools and also considering the aims and objectives of research.

3.5.4 Primary and Secondary data collection tools employed in research

In this particular research primary data has been collected through a questionnaire survey. Open ended questionnaire is prepared for this purpose. All the questions included in questionnaire are directed towards the aims and objectives of research. Interviews and focus group discussions are not employed because they are time consuming and costly. These two tools could not be incorporated effectively for collecting data in short time. Survey tool is also aligned with the research design and triangulation methodology. Through this tool, consumers of the Sainsbury will be targeted for collecting primary data.

Secondary data regarding consumer behavior and social class has been employed in this research through books, journals, articles and internet. While collecting secondary data from internet sources, only reliable resources have been used.

3.6 Population and Sample

Population of research comprises of all individuals on whom research is based. Population of this research is composed of all customers of Sainsbury in United Kingdom. Due to limited time and financial resources it was difficult for the researcher to collect primary data from whole population. To resolve this issue a sample gas been selected as representative part of population. Sample of research saves time and provides convenience in data collection (Ken, 2009). There are different techniques of selecting sample. These are probability sampling and non probability sampling techniques. In probability sampling all members of population are given chance to be selected in the sample whereas in non probability sampling technique all members are not given equal chance for being included in population (Struwig and Stead, 2007). Probability sampling techniques are not employed because they are very complicated and time consuming. In this particular research, sample of 75 customers of Sainsbury has been selected through convenience sampling which is technique of non probability sampling. Researcher has selected sample as per his convenience.

3.7 Validity and Reliability of Research

Correctness of research instrument measures validity of research (Jacobsen, 2002). If research instrument measures quantity for which research is aimed, research is a valid research. This particular research is conducted with the help of aligned methodology which aims at finding answer of research questions. All the questions in research instrument (questionnaire) have been focussed at the research aims and objectives. This contributes in making research a valid piece of work. Reliable sources have been employed for data collection. If a research produces consistent results, research is said to be a reliable research (Charles, 1995). This particular research has been conducted with consistent methodology which produces consistent results.

3.8 Research Ethics

Ethics are very important to be considered in every field. Research has been conducted by considering all important ethical issues. During data collection, researcher has not harmed any participant either emotionally or physically. It is unethical to harm any participant by any mean (Kimmel, 2007). Before data collection, all participants had been asked their free will to participate in the research. All the participants were informed about purpose of data collection. They were elaborated about aims and objectives of research. Researcher had ensured the respondents about confidentiality of data provided. Very important ethical issue considered in the research is that of plagiarism. Researcher has not copied or cheated work of any other author or researcher. In literature review secondary data has been employed which is work of previous researchers. In order to support secondary data, references have been provided in text as well as in bibliography. Furthermore researcher has not manipulated data during analysis.

3.9 Method of Data Analysis

Data collected from questionnaire survey has been analyzed descriptively. All the findings have been presented in the form of graphs. Researcher has conducted detailed discussion on the findings and related them with the secondary data. In this way relation between primary and secondary data has been established.

3.10 Summary of Chapter

Accurate methodology is very important for any research in order to find accurate results of research. This research has been through phenomenology philosophy of research which investigates beliefs and perceptions of people of society. Aligned with research philosophy, deductive and inductive approaches are employed in this particular research. Research has employed triangulation methods in order to find influence of social class on consumer behavior. Qualitative methods have been employed during construction of literature review whereas quantitative methods have been employed to analyze influence of social class on consumer behavior of Sainsbury. To collect primary data questionnaire survey has been used. A sample of 75 customers of Sainsbury is selected through convenience sampling technique. This chapter also discusses issues of validity and reliability of research.

Chapter Four
Data Findings and Presentation

4.1 Introduction

Data has been collected through a questionnaire survey. Response rate of 100% has been achieved in survey. In this chapter data findings are presented in a systematic way. All the findings are presented in the form of percentages. Graphical representation of data is also shown.

4.2 Data Findings

In the first stage general information of respondents has been presented. In the later stage data regarding social class and consumer behavior in Sainsbury has been presented.

4.2.1 General Information

In the general information age, gender and occupation of respondents have been presented. This information is asked from respondents because consumer behavior differs on the basis of age, gender and occupation of consumers. Marketers can find ways to design specific products and services for consumers belonging to a particular age, occupation and gender.

Gender:

Respondents were asked about their gender. There were 47% males and 53% females in sample. Sample was selected by convenience sampling and no distinction or priority was made for selecting males or females. Following is the data presentation of gender distribution of respondents:

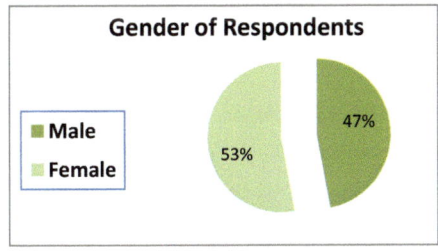

Major portion of graph represents females whereas smaller part represents males that were included in the sample.

Age:

Respondents were asked to mention their age range. The data findings show that there were 12% respondents who were less than 20 years. 30 % respondents belonged to age category of 21 – 30 years. In the age limit of 31 – 40 years, there were 26% respondents. 21% respondents were between the age limit of 41 to 50 years. Only 11 % respondents were above 50 years old. Overall data suggests that most of the respondents were in middle age category. Individuals belonging to different ages have different needs, preferences and attitudes. In simple words consumer behavior varies across different age limits. Graphical representation of results is as follows:

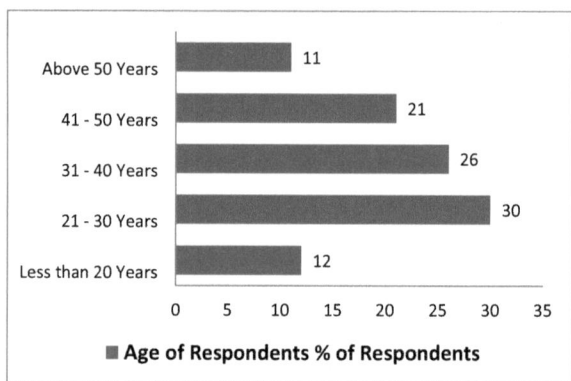

On x axis percentage of respondents has been taken and on y axis age limits have been taken. It is clear from graph that longest bar represents the individuals between the age limits of 21 to 30 years. The smallest bar represents the individuals who were above 50 years old. The other two long bar represent the individuals that were between the ages of 31 to 50 years.

Occupation

Individuals belonging to different social classes have different occupations and ultimately their preferences and attitudes also vary according to profession. Respondents were asked to mention the occupation to which they belonged. Data findings show that out of 75 respondents 11 % were factory workers, 12% were agriculture, and 24% were businessmen and 21% were shop owners.

Only 17% respondents were professionals, 9% were industrialists, and 4% were landlords. Only 2% were engaged in occupations other than the described above. Graphical representation of results is as follows:

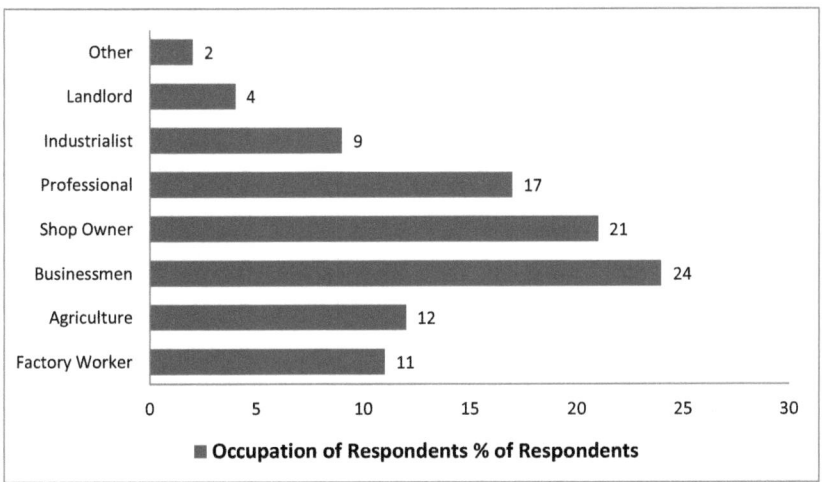

On x axis percentage of respondents has been taken. Y axis represents the occupations of individuals. It can be seen that most of the respondents were shop owners, industrialists, professionals, or businessmen. After this category, there were agriculturalists or factory workers. Then there is the category of landlords which is very short as compared to the other categories. In United Kingdom, social classes are defined on the basis of occupation and income. In this particular research, social classes of customers of Sainsbury are classified on the basis of occupation. Professionals, businessmen, shop owners and industrialists are categorized as middle or working class. Agriculturalists and factory workers are categorized as lower class and landlords are classified as upper class.

Question 1:

Respondents were asked that to which category major proportion of their income was allocated. Respondents belonging to different social classes have different attitudes and needs. Their total budget allocation differs from other individuals of other social classes. Marketers can take important details of budget allocation of individual of different social classes in order to design products that can match their needs. Data findings show that 33 % respondents said that major proportion of their income is allocated at food. 19% respondents said that major proportion of their income is taken by clothes. 27% respondents allocate major portion of their income to education. 9% respondents said that they allocate major portion of their income to luxuries. Entertainment was selected by 12% respondents. It has been found that respondents who belonged to lower class spend major proportion of their income on food. Respondents who belonged to middle or working class spend major proportion of their income either on food or education. Upper social class spends major proportion of their income on entertainment and luxuries. Graphical representation of data is as follows:

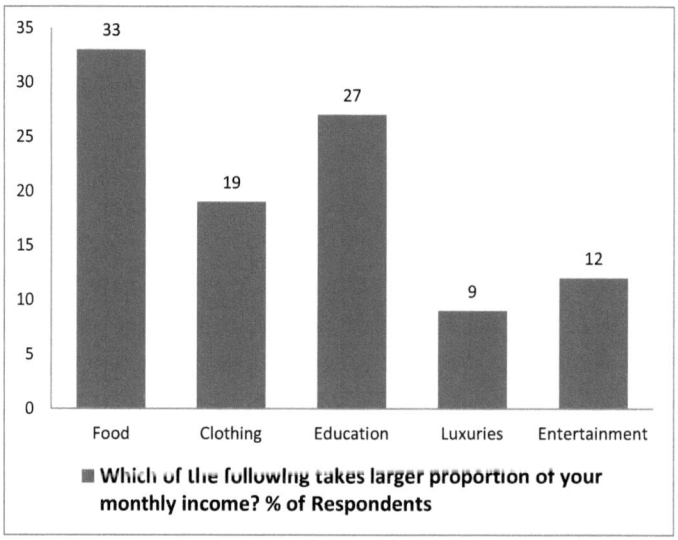

Y axis represents the percentage of respondents whereas x axis represents the items on which income is to be spent. The longest bar belongs to lower and middle class where people spend most of their incomes on necessities of life. On the other hand, the bars of 'luxuries' and 'entertainment' belong to upper class that has enough household income that can be spent on these activities. Marketers can offer necessities to the lower and middle classes at low price and they can also attract this segment towards entertainment by offering low prices.

Question 2:

Respondents were asked about the frequency of shopping. It depends on income and lifestyle of individuals that how frequently they shop from Sainsbury. 33% respondents said that they shop once a month from Sainsbury. 29 % respondents shop twice a month from Sainsbury. There were 25% respondents who shop once a week. 13% respondents shop twice a week. It has been found that respondents who belonged to lower or middle class have attitude of sopping once a month or twice a month. Respondents, who belonged to upper class, shop frequently from Sainsbury. Furthermore, respondents working fulltime shop once a month. Graphical representation of results is as follows:

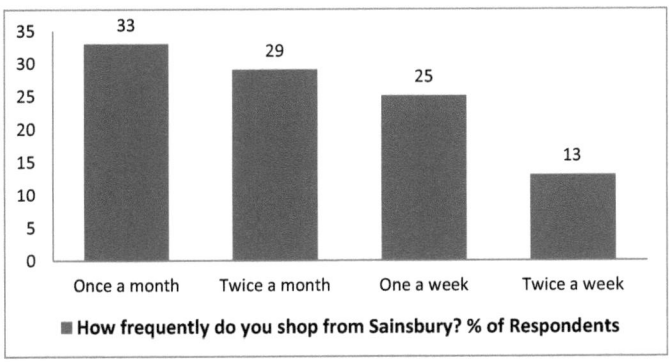

Y axis represents the percentage of respondents whereas x axis represents frequency of shopping. Individuals of lower and lower middle class shop once a month whereas the respondents who belonged to upper class shop either twice a week or once a week. This information is very valuable for marketers. They can offer special shopping offers to lower class in affordable range.

Question3:

Respondents were asked that whether they purchase durable goods or non durable goods frequently form Sainsbury. Durable goods are those goods that remain for a long time period whereas non durables are consumed after their purchase. Food, clothes or other products that fall in necessities are considered as non durable goods whereas luxuries e.g. home and car etc are durable goods. The results show that 45% respondents said that they frequently buy durable goods whereas 55% respondents said that they frequently buy non durable goods from

Sainsbury. The respondents belonging to upper middle and upper class spend large part of their income on durables whereas respondents belonging to lower middle and lower class spend large part of their income on nondurables. Graphical representation of results is as follows:

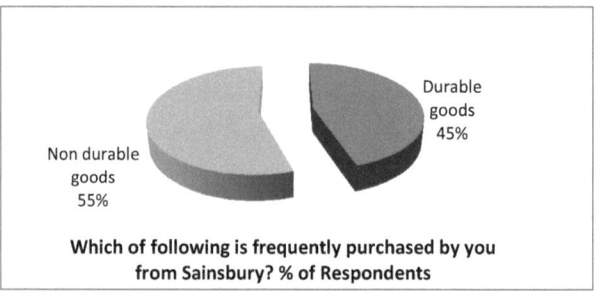

Which of following is frequently purchased by you from Sainsbury? % of Respondents

The above pie graph represents the results of question. Major part represents lower and middle classes which spend income on nondurables whereas the smaller part represents upper middle and upper classes which spend their income on durables such as home and vehicle.

Question 4:

Respondents were asked that whether they prefer to buy canned food form Sainsbury or not. Preference of individuals for canned or healthy food varies across different social classes. The results will enable to understand the food preferences of social classes. The data findings show that 14% respondents strongly agreed that they prefer canned food. 25% respondents agreed, 11 % remained neutral, 31% disagreed and 19% respondents strongly disagreed that they prefer canned food. Respondents belonging to upper classes tend to buy canned food where respondents belonging to lower class strongly disagreed to the fact that they buy canned food. Graphical representation of data findings is as follows:

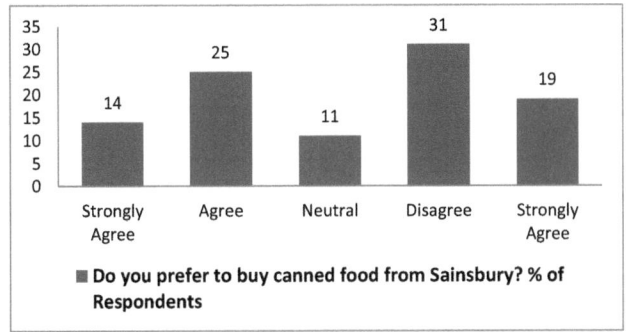

Y axis represents the percentage of respondents whereas x axis represents the scale for question ranging from strongly agree to strongly disagree. It has been found that upper classes prefer canned food whereas lower middle and middle classes did not prefer canned food of Sainsbury.

Question 5:

Respondents were asked that whether they prefer to buy branded alcoholic drinks from Sainsbury or not. Preferences for purchasing brands differ across different social classes. Individuals of upper class have more exposure to branded item as compared to that of lower social classes. The data findings show that 13% respondents strongly agreed that they prefer branded alcoholic drinks. 28% respondents agreed, 9 % remained neutral, 34% disagreed and 16% respondents strongly disagreed that they prefer branded alcoholic drinks. Respondents belonging to upper or upper middle classes preferred to buy branded alcoholic drinks where respondents belonging to lower class strongly disagreed to the fact that they buy branded alcoholic drinks. Graphical representation of data findings is as follows:

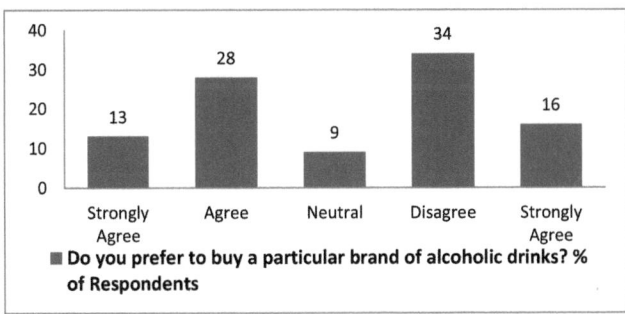

Y axis represents the percentage of respondents whereas x axis represents the scale for question ranging from strongly agree to strongly disagree. In this graph lower class and lower middle class disagreed to prefer branded alcoholic drinks whereas upper classes agreed to prefer branded drinks.

Question6:

Respondents were asked that whether they give importance to clothing brands or not. Clothing is a necessity and every one whether he/she is in upper, middle or lower class wants it. Difference comes in the choice of materials and brands of clothing. The results show that out of 75 respondents, 13% respondents strongly agreed that they give high level importance to branded clothes. 26% agreed, 14% remained neutral, 35% disagreed and 12% strongly disagreed to the opinion that they give high level importance to branded clothes. It has been found that respondents of upper class strongly agreed that they give high level importance to branded clothes and respondents of upper middle class agreed to this opinion. On the other hand respondents of lower class do not give high level importance to branded clothes. They strongly disagreed with this opinion. Graphical representation of findings is as follows:

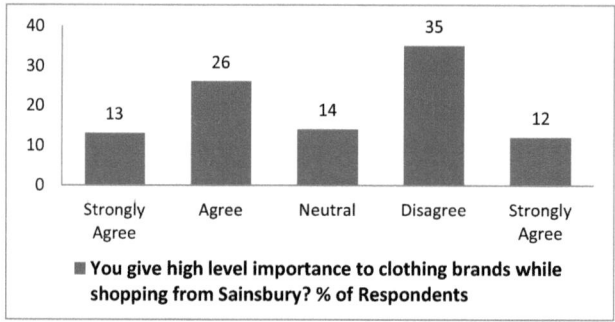

Y axis represents the percentage of respondents whereas x axis represents the scale for question ranging from strongly agree to strongly disagree. In this graph, lower class and lower middle class are represented by 'disagree' and 'strongly disagree' columns whereas upper middle and upper classes are represented by 'strongly agree' or 'agree' columns. Marketers can offer each segment with appropriate offers in affordable ranges.

Question 7:

Respondents were asked about the fact that whether fashionable styles are at their priority while shopping clothes or not. As discussed earlier that clothing is necessity so everyone wants this. It depends on priority of individuals that whether they simply fulfill their need or desire something more. As far as findings are concerned, 19% respondents strongly agreed that fashionable clothes are at their priority when they purchase clothes. 27% agreed, 13% remained neutral, 30% disagreed and 11% strongly disagreed with this opinion. Findings suggest that respondents of upper class strongly agreed that they give high level priority to fashionable clothes. Respondents belonging to upper middle class have same kind of attitude but with low intensity. On the other hand respondents of lower class do not give high level priority to fashionable clothes; they fulfill their need with simple clothes. Graphical representation of findings is as follows:

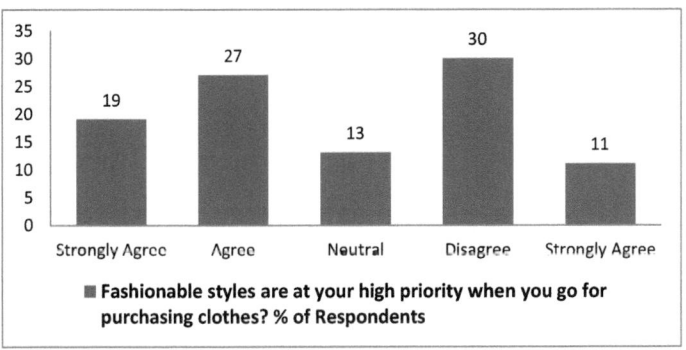

Y axis represents the percentage of respondents whereas x axis represents the scale for question ranging from strongly agree to strongly disagree. Marketers can attract the upper classes with unique fashionable clothes that prioritize fashionable clothes. On the other hand, lower classes can also be attracted to fashionable clothes in affordable price range.

Question 8:

Individuals belonging to different social classes have different attitudes and preferences for visiting restaurants. It depends on the budget of individuals that how much they can spend on restaurants. This question was asked to find that whether they go outside to eat most of the time or eat at home. This data can assist marketers for satisfying customers' food needs. Customers who cannot go outside because of money constraints can be provided with the same quality and taste at their homes. The findings suggest that 15% respondents have very high frequency of going at restaurants. 26% respondents have high, 16 % moderate, 29% low and 14% respondents have very low frequency of visits to restaurants. It has been found that respondents belonging to lower class have very low frequency of visiting restaurants. Lower middle class has low frequency of visiting restaurants whereas upper and upper middle classes have high frequency of visiting restaurants. Graphical representation of data findings are as follows:

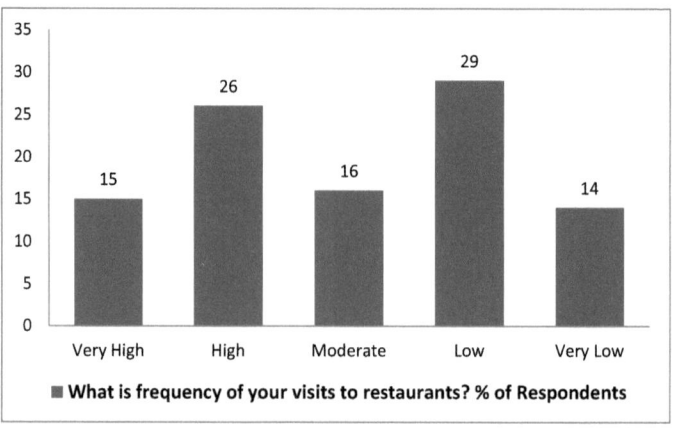

Y axis represents the percentage of respondents whereas x axis represents the scale for question ranging from very high to very low. In this graph, lower class was represented by 'very low' column, upper class by 'high' and middle class by 'moderate' columns. Marketers have very strong implications regarding this information. Lower classes can be offered with the food that has taste of food of restaurants. Marketers can also attract upper classes towards healthy food by special offers.

Question 9:

Respondents were asked about their activity in leisure time. Social classes differ in their activities of leisure time. Marketers can catch customers at sites where they are found in their leisure time. As far as answers of respondents are concerned, 23% said that they spend their leisure time in visiting friends, 32% respondents spend their leisure time in sports, and 29 %

respondents spend their leisure time in theaters and concerts. There were 16% respondents who spend their leisure time in other activities. It has been found that lower middle class and middle class spend their time in visiting friends. Upper middle class spend their time in sports and visiting friends and other activities. Respondents belonging to upper class spend their leisure time in theatres and concerts. Graphical representation of data findings are as follows:

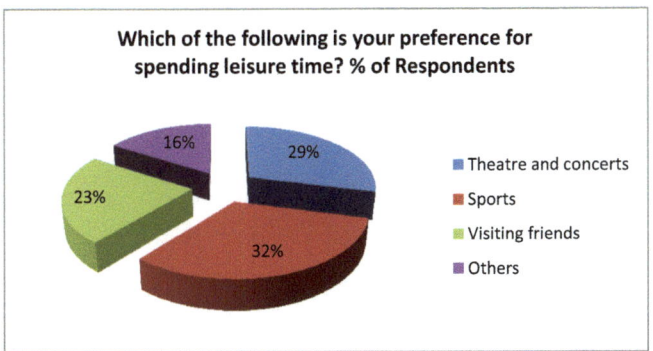

This pie graph represents the spending of leisure time in different activities. The major portion represents sports, blue portion represents theatres and concerts, green portion represents visiting friends and purple portion represents some other activities.

Question 10:

Respondents were asked that from which source they get information about the products and services of Sainsbury. Different social classes have varying access to communication media. Usually, modern means of communication are available to upper class only. Marketers can target customers according to the media source which is available and accessible to them. Data findings show that 32% respondents get information about the products and services of company through newspaper. 28% respondents get information through magazines, and 24% respondents get information through television. There were only 16% respondents who get information about the products and services of company through internet. Respondents belonging to upper and upper middle class have access to internet whereas respondents belonging to lower class have ease on getting information through newspapers. Graphical representation of findings is as follows:

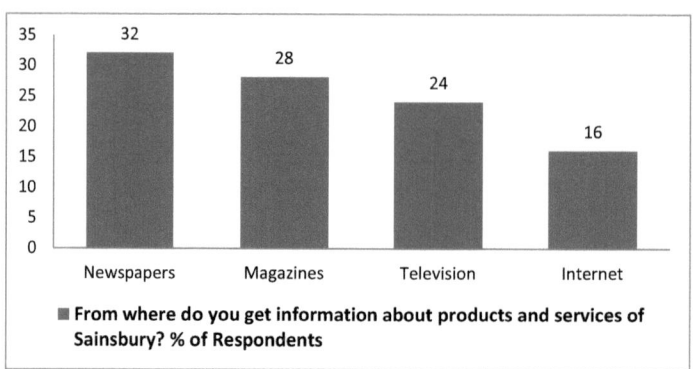

From where do you get information about products and services of Sainsbury? % of Respondents

Y axis represents the percentage of respondents whereas x axis represents modes of communication. Respondents who belonged to lower classes get information through 'newspaper' and respondents belonging to upper class get information about the offers of company through 'internet'. This information is of high value for marketers who can target specific social class with appropriate communication media. Lower and lower middle classes can be targeted through 'newspapers' and 'television' whereas upper classes can be targeted through 'internet'.

Question 11:

Online shopping is becoming very famous in the modern era. Internet is modern mean of communication. Respondents were asked about their preference of online shopping over physical shopping. Data findings show that 18% respondents strongly agreed that they prefer online shopping over physical shopping. There were 21% respondents who agreed that they prefer online shopping over physical shopping. These respondents belonged to upper middle class and upper class. 15% respondents remained neutral in their response. 32% respondents disagreed and 14 % respondents strongly disagreed that they prefer online shopping over physical shopping. These respondents belonged to lower middle and lower classes. Graphical representation of data findings is as follows:

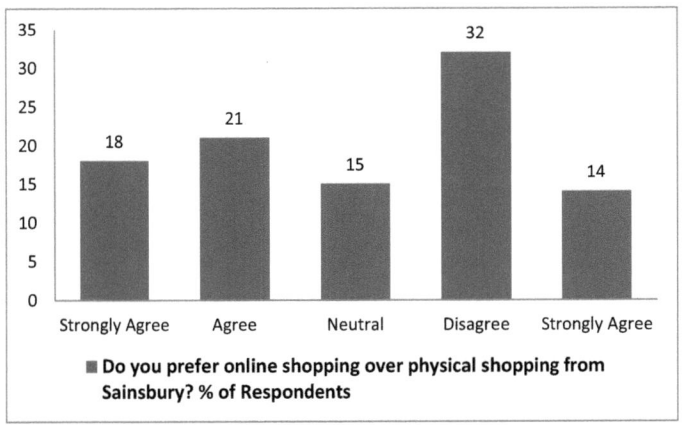

Y axis represents the percentage of respondents whereas x axis represents the scale for question ranging strongly agree to strongly disagree. In the above graph, respondents of lower and lower middle class are represented by 'disagree' and 'strongly disagree' column whereas respondents of upper class are represented by 'strongly agree' and 'agree' column. The products which belong to upper classes can be offered online. On the other hand, marketers can also attract other social classes (lower class and middle class) towards online shopping by offering low prices on online stores.

Question 12:

Respondents were asked about the financial products availed by them from Sainsbury's bank. Individuals belonging to different social classes adopt different financial strategies for themselves depending upon their budgets. It has been found through data findings that 23% respondents said that they invest in insurance frequently. These respondents belonged to middle class specifically. There were 17% respondents who preferred to invest in real estate and 20% respondents preferred to invest in stocks. These respondents belonged to upper middle and upper classes. There were 18% respondents who have availed credit cards and 22 % respondents have taken bank loans. These respondents belonged to either lower or lower middle class. Graphical representation of data findings is as follows:

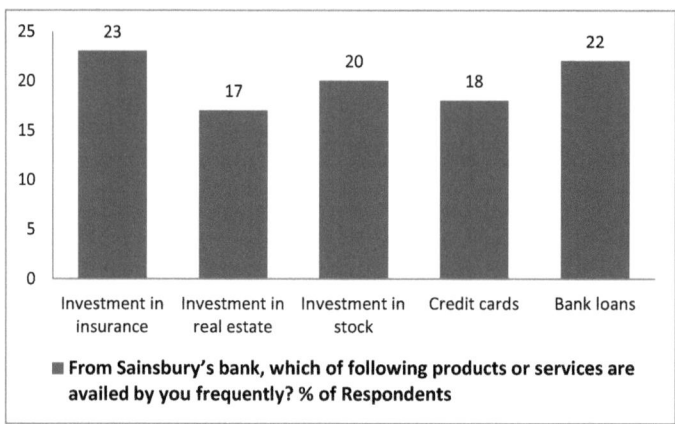

Y axis represents the percentage of respondents whereas x axis represents different financial measures taken by respondents. Respondents belonging to lower classes are represented by columns of 'credit cards' and 'bank loans'. On the other hand, respondents belonging to upper and upper middle class belong to the columns of investment in stock, investment in real estate.

4.3 Chapter Summary

This chapter has presented data findings in the form of graphs and text. Data has been converted into percentages and presented in the form of graphs. Each question is related to the social classes so that aims and objectives can be achieved. This chapter has presented data, no analysis is done here. In the next chapter all these findings are discussed in detail to reach at conclusion.

Chapter Five
Data Interpretation and Analysis

5.1 Introduction

Research has been conducted to evaluate the influence of social class on consumer behavior in Sainsbury. Data has been collected through a questionnaire survey from a sample of 75 consumers has been selected through convenience sampling. In the previous chapter data collected through research tool has been presented. This chapter analyses the data collected through questionnaire. Descriptive method of data analysis has been used for analyzing the findings of research.

5.2 Analysis of findings

Respondents were asked about the age and data shows that there were 47 % males and 52 % females in the sample. The findings suggest that the customer population of Sainsbury has more females as compared to males. People belonging to different age categories have different attitudes. In different social classes individuals of different ages have different perceptions, beliefs and attitudes. It was found that most of the respondents were between the age categories of 20 to 40 years.

5.2.1 Social Class Breakdown

Different social classes have different occupations and interests. Social classes of the respondents were categorized on the basis of occupation. It was found that majority of respondents belonged to middle or working class. The second major category was of lower class whereas the least category was of upper class. This is consistent with the facts that in United Kingdom, majority of the individuals belong to working class. Upper class is associated with high income and pool of resources whereas lower classes have limited resources. This is basically due to the differences in occupations of individuals in different social classes. Respondents who were either professionals, businessmen, shop owners or businessmen were categorized as working or middle class. On the other hand, factory workers and agriculturalists were placed in lower class and landlords were placed in upper class. This social stratification of customers of Sainsbury is consistent with social stratification of United Kingdom (www.woodlands-junior.kent.sch.uk/customs/questions/class.htm).

5.2.2 Consumption preference for Food and Entertainment

The differences in consumption patterns were also found through survey results. It has been found that most of the respondents spend their large proportion of income on food. The second major category that takes major portion of income of respondents was cloth. Entertainment takes less proportion of income of respondents. It has been found that most of the respondents who belonged to middle or lower classes spend majority of income on food. These findings are consistent with the findings of Arnold (2002) who says that respondents who belong to lower classes or middle classes spend major portion of income on necessities of life e.g. food and shelter. The survey results showed that respondents belonging to lower or middle social classes spend large portion of their income on necessities. Lower social classes have low income which is spent on fulfilling necessities of life. On the other hand it was found the respondents who belonged to upper classes spend their income on activities like entertainment and luxuries. This information has important marketing implications. Marketers can design different offers for different social classes. Respondents belonging to lower and middle social classes can be offered economical packages of food products. Upper classes can be targeted with more entertainment oriented products by the marketers. Thus, it is clear that social class stratification has impact on the consumption patterns of the consumers. This is very valuable information for the marketers who can offer different products for upper, middle and lower classes on the basis of their consumption patterns. If marketers of Salisbury try to attract lower classes with entertainment products, they would be doing wrong as lower class does not have enough pool of resources for spending on entertainment and luxuries.

5.2.3 Frequency of Shopping

It was found that most of the respondents shop once a month and a small percentage of individuals tend to shop twice a week from Sainsbury. The respondents who were working fulltime usually shop once a week. Two reasons can be associated with this fact. One is that respondents working fulltime have less time for shopping so they buy once a month from Sainsbury. These people usually buy from in bulk quantities in order to avail discounts. Second reason is that respondents having low income shop less frequently due to income constraints.

Albert and David (1993) have also found that lower and middle social classes shop less frequently as compared to upper classes. Marketers can use this information for targeting different social classes. Lower and middle class can be offered economical packages having large quantity with discounts. On the other hand upper social class can be offered with differentiated products because this social class shops frequently and to maintain its interest in shopping differentiation is important. Thus, it can be deduced that the social classes differ in their frequency of shopping. Marketers of Sainsbury can have very strong implications of frequency of shopping for granting discounted packages or differentiated products to different social classes.

5.2.4 Preference for Buying Durables and Nondurables

It has been found that majority of respondents spend their income on nondurables. Nondurables include food and clothing. Durables can be classified under luxuries. Food is most important component of nondurables. The survey results also show that major proportion of income of lower and middle classes is spent on food. The findings suggest that respondents belonging to lower of lower middle class spend income on nondurables. This information can be used by marketers for promoting durables and nondurable goods. The results of survey also showed that upper middle and middle classes spend major part of their income on durables such homes and vehicles. This is due to the fact that lower and middle classes do not have enough disposable income, so they cannot afford durables out of their less income. As it is found that lower and middle classes do not spend their income on durables, so marketers can attract these social classes towards durables by offering discounts and low prices. Thus, it can be deduced that different social classes differ in their consumption on durables and nondurables. Middle and lower classes do not have enough income for gaining durables, so they spent their income on nondurables. On the other hand, upper class can spend large percentage of income on luxuries and durables. Sainsbury offers a wide range of nondurables and also significant portion f durables to its customers. Marketers can target specific social classes for durables and nondurables.

5.2.5 Preference for Buying Branded, Non-branded and Fashionable Products

Branded, canned and healthy diet is associated to the high class. Food is the necessity of life that is required by everyone in all social classes. Individuals have differences in the selection of food items depending on the social class. It has been found that most of the respondents did not prefer canned food from Sainsbury. Canned food is usually expensive as compared to non canned food. The results of research show that lower classes did not prefer canned food whereas upper classes prefer canned food to a high level. Mirela (2006) has also found in his research that upper class tends to buy healthy and canned food. His findings suggested that upper classes prefer to buy macrobiotic food as compared whereas lower and middle classes do not prefer to have canned food. Marketers can incorporate this information while designing food items for different social classes. Keiser and Kuehl (1972) found that there is relationship between brand identification and social classes. Upper social classes tend to prefer brands because they want to satisfy their cognitive self image. In accordance with this fact, it has been found that most of the respondents of lower and lower middle classes do not prefer to buy branded alcoholic drinks from Sainsbury. Brands are preferred by the respondents who have high income.

It has been found that most of the respondents did not give importance to brands of clothes while shopping. The respondents who belonged to upper classes give more importance to brands and quality of clothes, whereas respondents who belonged to lower classes did not prefer branded clothes. Mirela (2006) takes this factor in a sense that lower classes give less importance to quality of clothes and consider about price to a high level. The respondents from lower social classes have less income so they cannot afford expensive branded clothes rather they prefer to buy simple clothes. Marketers can target each social class on the basis of its preference for clothing. Upper social class can be targeted with fashionable and differentiated clothes at high prices. On the other hand, lower and middle social classes can be offered less fashionable but quality clothes at low prices.

When asked about fashionable styles of clothes, majority disagreed that they prefer to buy fashionable clothes. These respondents either belonged to lower or lower middle classes. On the other hand a considerable percentage of respondents of upper classes agreed to have fashionable clothes while shopping clothes. It suggests that gender and status level both have impact on respondents' intentions for fashionable clothes. It has been found that upper middle and some lower middle class respondents also consider fashionable clothes while shopping. This can be related to trickledown effect in which lower classes copy the buying behavior of upper class in terms of fashionable clothes (Noel, 2008). This information can be very valuable for the marketers for offering fashionable and branded products to different social classes.

Thus, it is deduced that social classes differ in their perceptions towards consumption of branded, non-branded and fashionable goods. Marketers can attract upper classes with branded and fashionable goods whereas lower and middle classes can be attracted towards non-branded but fashionable goods.

5.2.6 Attitude of Visiting Restaurants

Respondents were asked about their frequency of visiting restaurants. It has been found that respondents who belonged to upper class have more frequency of visiting restaurants. On the other hand respondents who have less frequency of visiting restaurants belonged to lower classes. Mirela (2006) has also found in his research that lower classes have less frequency of visiting restaurants. The aim of asking this question was to analyze the preference of customers for having food from outside house. The results have shown that lower middle and lower social classes prefer to eat at homes whereas upper social class prefers to go to restaurants. This analysis can assist marketers of Sainsbury to analyze preference of food of its consumers. Although lower classes have low frequency of going outside for eating, yet they have desire of eating tasty food. Marketers can design less costly food products for such customers that can satisfy their desire of eating outside.

Thus, respondents of different social classes also differ in their frequency of visiting restaurants. Marketers of Sainsbury can attract working class with canned food at reasonable prices because this class does not have enough time for cooking food at home. Cooked food in cans or easy to cook food can be offered to working class with reasonable prices. On the other hand, lower class can be attracted with raw food because respondents of this class prefer to eat at home by cooking themselves.

5.2.7 Leisure Activities

It has been found that lower classes spend their leisure time in visiting friends and sports activities. A large proportion of middle class respondents spend its leisure time in sport activities and at concerts. Upper class spends in time in visiting theatres and sports clubs. Data findings show that upper class spends its time in sophisticated activities whereas lower classes spend their leisure time in general activities for which they do not have time in usual working e.g. visiting friends. Marketers of Sainsbury can catch consumers at places where they are found in their leisure time. Burdge (1969) has also found that social classes differ from each other in respect of spending their leisure time. It also depends on the lifestyle and preferences of consumers that where do they prefer to spend their leisure time. Mirela (2006) has found that upper classes spend their leisure time in theatres, concerts and restaurants whereas lower classes spend their time in sports. Thus, it is deduced from the data findings that social classes differ in their leisure activities. This information can be very valuable for the marketers of the Sainsbury. They can target specific social classes at the particular areas or places where individuals of each social class spend leisure time. The data findings imply that upper classes can be attracted at theaters, golf and tennis clubs because they are interested in visiting theaters and doing sports. On the other hand, middle class can be targeted at concerts and sports clubs.

5.2.8 Preference for Communication Media Type

Respondents were asked about the way through which they get information about products and services of company. Schiffman, L.G., & Kanuk (2007) have argued that social classes differ in choosing the medium through which they can get information. The same thing has been observed in the findings of this particular research. It has been found that respondents who belonged to lower classes are more familiar with newspaper and television. Middle class relies on televisions and magazines for getting information about products and services of company. Upper class respondents rely on internet for getting information about products and services of company. It suggests that communication strategies of social classes differ depending upon the income level. Newspapers and television are less costly methods of communication so they are availed by lower classes. Internet is modern and costly mean of communication as compared to other means of communication so it is availed by consumers having high income and education level. In specific terms, it was found that professionals and businessmen were more interested in internet, so marketers of Sainsbury can attract this particular group of working class through online sources. On the other hand, agriculturalists and factory workers prefer to read newspapers, so they can be attracted through magazines and newspapers. Landlords were found to be interested in online shopping, so they can also be attracted through online media.

5.2.9 Preference for Online Shopping

Further respondents were asked about the preference of channel for shopping. There are two types of main media for shopping. These are physical shopping and online shopping. Data findings show that a large percentage does not prefer online shopping over physical shopping. The respondents who belonged to middle classes do not prefer online shopping over physical shopping. On the other hand respondents belonging to upper class prefer to go for online shopping. This is because of differences in income and knowledge and education level of different social classes. Respondents belonging to lower class have limited knowledge of internet and computer so they do not select internet shopping whereas respondents belonging to upper classes have high knowledge of internet so they prefer online shopping. Smith and Rupp (2003) have found that lower classes have fewer intentions towards online shopping as compared to that of upper classes. Intentions for online shopping also depend on convenience. If consumers feel convenience in using internet media, online shopping intentions would be higher. Agriculturalists and factory workers do not have enough knowledge of computer and online media so it will not be worthwhile to attract this social class to online shopping. On the other hand, professionals and businessmen have knowledge and experience of using computer and internet, so they can be targeted for online shopping.

5.2.10 Preference for Financial Products

Finally respondents were asked about their attitude of spending towards different financial products. It has been found that most of the respondents take investment in insurance. These respondents belonged to middle class who want to secure their future. There was least number of respondents who preferred to take investment in real estate. These respondents were either businessmen or landlords. Respondents who preferred to invest in stocks also belonged to upper and middle class. The respondents who preferred to invest in bank loans and credit cards belonged to lower classes. It has been deduced from the findings that lower classes tend to take loan for meeting their expenses. They can be agriculturalists or factory workers who take loan for meeting big expenses such as irrigation of land etc. Lower class tends to spend today and pay later. This is because lower and middle classes follow trickledown effect that allows respondents to spend money. Mathews and Slocum (1969) say that lower classes have tendency to take credit and upper class has tendency to invest in profitable projects. Same has been found in this particular research. Overall results suggest that there are differences in the financial planning of different social classes. This information is very valuable in terms of marketing. The respondents of upper social classes can be targeted with investment opportunities whereas lower classes can be attracted with loan schemes and credit card offers.

The analysis of findings suggests that most of the respondents belonged to lower or lower middle class. Different social classes have different professions and different nature of spending in different products. Overall, differences have been recognized in the consumption patterns of lower, middle and upper classes of United Kingdom.

5.3 Summary of Chapter

Overall results of data analysis show that different social classes have differences in their consumer behavior. Occupation, spending of food, clothes, spending on branded products, frequency of shopping and attitude towards fashionable products vary. Furthermore there are differences in the social classes about selecting medium for shopping i.e. online or physical. Leisure activities of different social classes also vary depending upon their occupation. There are also differences in modes of communication and financial planning in different social classes. Simply it can be deduced that consumer behavior of different social classes vary.

Chapter Six
Conclusion and Recommendations

6.1 Introduction

Data findings have been analyzed in detail in the previous section. This section is going to conclude the results of the research. All important points related to social class and consumer behavior have been concluded. On the basis of findings implications of research have also been proposed. Further the limitations of research and future research aspects are also presented at the end of this section.

6.2 Conclusion

It has been concluded from the findings of research that social classes do have influence on consumer behavior. Attitude, preferences, beliefs, and behaviors of individuals of different social classes differ from each other. The objectives of this research are reviewed as follows:

- Different social classes have different attitudes of consumption. It is concluded that most of the respondents were industrialist, professionals, shop owners or businessmen who fall in middle or working class. The second major class was found lower class which included agriculturalists or factory workers. Upper class was very short and composed of landlords only.

- It is concluded that lower, upper and middle classes differ in their consumer behavior because of changes in education and income level. Lower class is less educated and has low income, so it spends only on necessities of life. On the other hand, middle or working class spends large portion of its income on education. They have attitudes of spending on brands and fashion but also have low income. So marketers can design cost effective brands and fashionable products for middle class. The upper class has enough pool of resources which can be spent on brands and fashionable products.

- One more conclusion drawn from findings is that middle class follows trickledown effect in fashionable goods. They follow the trends of upper class but their budget does not allow them to purchase expensive products. Marketers can use this information for designing cost effective products for satisfying middle class.

- From the findings of research it has been concluded that lower class has less frequency of visiting restaurants. This can be because of fewer resources possessed by lower class. This shows the preference of consumers for eating outside home. Upper classes have found to be frequently visiting restaurants. These findings can be very helpful for the marketing of Sainsbury for satisfying consumers by providing them different food products. Through the findings it has also been concluded that lower classes spend their leisure time in visiting friends and sports activities. On the other hand upper classes spend their leisure time in visiting theatres and concerts.

- The ways through which different social classes communicate and receive information about products and services of Sainsbury differ. It has been concluded that television and newspaper are good sources of communication for lower and middle classes whereas internet has found to be a good source of communication for upper classes. From findings of research it has been concluded that upper class tends to experience online shopping. Lower classes have more intentions for shopping from physical stores of Sainsbury.

- Finally it has been concluded that social classes differ in their financial planning. Lower classes have more tendencies of taking loan and shopping through credit cards whereas upper classes have more attitude of investing in stocks and real-estate. Marketers can have important implications of the findings of research. Behavior and attitude of each social class must be considered by the marketers for targeting each class. Following conclusions are made on the basis of findings of research:

  ✓ Majority of population of Sainsbury's consumers is composed of middle class
  ✓ Upper classes are more conscious of food quality, brands of clothes, and fashionable styles. Upper class frequently shops from Sainsbury. This class has more intentions of online shopping and investments in profitable projects.
  ✓ Lower classes shop less frequently and are not conscious of brands and quality. They prefer to go for physical shopping. Bank loan and use of credit cards has been frequent in this particular class.

- ✓ Middle class follows trends of upper classes in shopping clothes and fashionable products in order to satisfy its cognitive self image.

6.3 Implications of Research

The results of research have number of implications for marketing of Sainsbury. Marketers need to consider the needs, preferences and attitudes of different social classes in order to provide them products and services that can satisfy their needs at utmost level. Income level of lower and middle classes is low as compared to upper social class. This income level directly affects their needs and preferences. Marketers can design can offer less costly and non branded food and clothes to lower classes. In order to attract customers of upper class branded products (food and clothes) can be designed. Lower and middle class shop less frequently and they seek for availing discounts on purchasing bulk quantities. Marketers can offer bulk packages to middle and lower classes because they shop less frequently and want to avail discounts. On the other hand marketers can work to offer distinct and differentiated products to upper class because they shop frequently. Purchasing again and again same kind of products can create dissatisfaction in upper class. To resolve this issue differentiation can be a suitable approach for products offered to upper social class. Lower and middle classes are more exposed to television and newspaper so to target them marketers can use these two modes of communication. Products related to lower class and middle class must be advertised on television and newspapers whereas products related to upper class must be advertised on internet media and magazines so that particular social class can easily get access to information related to company's offerings. On the other hand upper class can be targeted through elite class magazines and internet. Marketers can plan for attracting upper class for online shopping. Moreover middle can also be attracted to online shopping by providing discounts on online shopping. Lower classes have low income but high desires. They can have intentions to buy today and pay tomorrow. Marketers can provide credits facility to these social classes. Sainsbury owns a bank and this information can be useful for marketing of its financial products. Individuals of Middle class can be targeted by insurance packages for persuading them to secure their future. Small loans can be granted to lower classes on suitable terms. On whole influence of social class on consumer behavior of Sainsbury has valuable marketing implications.

6.4 Limitations

Research has been conducted with limited resources and time. Time constraint was major limitation of this particular research. Findings of research have been limited to the data provided by the participants. Although response rate of 100% has been received in this particular research yet the quality and truthfulness on the part of participants van be questionable. Findings of research are limited to the responses of participants only. This particular research has been limited to Sainsbury only. Only marketing implications are considered by the researcher. A small sample has been used for this particular research so its findings cannot be generalized.

6.5 Future Research

Research can be extended by future researchers. This research has been conducted on a sample of 75 consumers of Sainsbury which can be increased by future researchers. Future researchers can take a larger sample and conduct the same research with same instrument. This could enable future researchers to extend the scope of this particular research. Research can also be extended by future researchers by adopting a different research instrument. New research instrument will bring different results for the same research questions.

References

Adela McMurray, (2004), Research: *a commonsense approach*, Cengage Learning Australia

Albert Loudon and David Della Britta, *Consumer Behavior* : Concepts and Applications, , McGraw Hill.

Blaikie, N. 2000, *Designing Social Research*, 1st ed, Polity Press, Cambridge.

Banerjee, R. and Batinit, N. 1993. *UK Consumer Habits,* Available at http://www.eea-esem.com/papers/eea-esem/2003/2199/UK_consumer_habits.pdf

Belch,G.E.,and Landon, E.L., 1977, Discriminate Validity of a Product. Anchored Self Concept Measure, *Journal of Marketing Research*, 14:252-56.

Catherine Marshall , Gretchen B. Rossman . 1999, *Designing Qualitative Researc,. 3rd Ed. Sage Publication Inc*

Easterby Smith, M., M. A. Lyles, et al. 2008. Inter organizational knowledge transfer. Current themes and future prospects. *Journal of Management Studies*

Garland, R., 2002. Non-financial drivers of customer profitability in personal retail banking. *Journal of Targeting, Measurement and Analysis in Marketing* 10 (3), 233-248.

Hodder Arnold, 2002, Cave S – Consumer Behaviour in a Week, ISBN 0340849711

Hatch, M. J. and Cunliffe, A. L. 2006, *Organization Theory*, 2nd ed, Oxford University Press, Oxford.

Husserl, E., 2001, *The Shorter Logical Investigations*. London and New York: Routledge

H. L. Mathews and J. W. Slocum, Jr., "Social Class and Commercial Bank Credit Card Usage," Journal of Marketing, 33 (January 1969), 71-78.

Ken Black, 2009. Business Statistics: *Contemporary Decision Making*. John Wiley and Sons, 6th Ed

Loudon. 2007. *Consumer Behavior.* 4th Ed. India: Tata McGraw Hill

Lantos, G. 2010. *Consumer Behavior in Action.* 1st Ed. USA: M.E. Sharpe Inc.

Loudon, 2001. Consumer Behavior: Concepts And Applications, Tata McGraw-Hill Education

Mihić Mirela and Gordana Čulina, 2006. Buying Behavior and Consumption: Social Class versus Income, Management, Vol. 11, 2006, 2, pp. 77-92

Michael R. Solomon, 2004, Consumer Behavior: Buying, Having, and Being, Ed 6th

Myers, J. H. Stanton, R. R. and Haug, A. F. 1971: Correlates of Buying Behavior: Social Class vs. Income, Journal of Marketing, Vol. 35, No 4; pp. 8–16.

Noel, H. 2009. *Consumer Behavior.* 1st Ed. USA: Ingram Publisher Services Inc

O'Doughtery, D. 2007. *Consumer Behavior.* 1st Ed. Cape Town: Catherine Rose

Pintrich, P. 2005. *Handbook of self regulation.* 2nd Ed. UK: Elsevier

Pantzis, C., Gordon, D. and Levitas, R. 2006. *Poverty and social exclusion in Britain.* 1st Ed. Great Britain: The Policy Press.

Pan, S. 2011 What is Social Research? WiseGEEK 2, pp.1-9.

P. Martineao, "Social Classes and Spending Behavior," Journal of Marketing, 23 (October 1958), 121-130.

Russ-Eft, D., & Preskill, H. 2001. *Evaluation in Organizations.* New York: Basic Books

Rookes, P. and Willson, J. 2000. *Perception.* 1st Ed. USA: Routledge

R. J. Burdge, "Levels of Occupational prestige and Leisure Activity," Journal of Leisure Research, 1 (Summer 1969), 262-274.

Solomon, 1996 consumer behaviour, 3rd edn Prentice Hall Englewood Cliffs. NJ , 33

Schhiffman J.B and Kanuk Lealie Lazar , 1997, *Consumer Behavior* published by Prentice Hall Sixth edition .446

Schiffman. 2007. *Consumer Behavior.* 9th Ed. India: Pearson Education Inc

Stephen K. Keiser, Philip G. Kuehl , 1972, "Social Class And Income Influences On External Search Processes Of Adolescents", in Proceedings of the Third Annual Conference of the Association for Consumer Research: Association for Consumer Research, Pages: 602-631.

S. J. Levy, 1966, "Social Class and Consumer Behavior," in Joseph W. Newman, ed., On Knowing the Consumer. New York: John Wiley and Sons

S. V. Rich and S. C. Jain, 1968,"Social Class and Life Cycle as Predictors of Shopping Behavior," Journal of Marketing Research, No 5 , 41-49.

Schaninger, Charles M. 1981, "Social Class vs. Income Revisited: An Empirical Investigation," Journal of

Schiffman, L.G., & Kanuk, L.L. 2007. Consumer Behavior, 9th ed. New Jersey, Pearson Prentice Hall.

Saunders, M., Lewis, P. and Thornhill, A. 2007, *Research Methods for Business Students*, 4th ed, Prentice Hall Financial Times, Harlow.

Saunders et al., 2009. *Research methods for business students*, Prentice Hall.

Struwig and Stead ,2007. *Planning, designing and reporting research*

Charles, C. M. 1995. Introduction to educational research 2nd ed.

Kimmel, A. 2007. Ethical Issues and Behavioral Research. 2nd Ed. UK: Blackwell Publishing.

Smith, D. A. and Rupp, T.W. 2003 'Strategic online customer decision making: leveraging the transformational power of the Internet', Online Information Review 27: 6, 418 – 432.

Wayne D. Hoyer , Deborah J. Macinnis, 2009, *Consumer Behavior*, Ed 5th

Young, B. 2003. Does food advertising influence children's food choices? A critical review of some of the recent literature. International Journal of Advertising, 22, pp. 441-459.

http://www.woodlands-junior.kent.sch.uk/customs/questions/class.htm

Questionnaire
General Information

Gender:

a) Male
b) Female

Age:

a) Less than 20 Years
b) 21 – 3O Years
c) 31 – 40 Years
d) 41 – 50 Years
e) Above 50 Years

What is your or your parent's Occupation?

a) Factory worker
b) Agriculture
c) Businessmen
d) Professional
e) Industrialist
f) Shop owner
g) Landlord
h) Other

1. Which of the following takes larger proportion of your monthly income?

a) Food
b) Clothing
c) Education
d) Luxuries
e) Entertainment

2. How frequently do you shop from Sainsbury?

a) Once a month
b) Twice a month
c) One a week

d) Twice a week

3. Which of following is frequently purchased by you from Sainsbury?

a) Durable goods

b) Non durable goods

4. Do you prefer to buy canned food from Sainsbury?

a) Strongly Agree

b) Agree

c) Neutral

d) Disagree

e) Strongly Agree

5. Do you prefer to buy a particular brand of alcoholic drinks?

a) Strongly Agree

b) Agree

c) Neutral

d) Disagree

e) Strongly Agree

6. You give high level importance to clothing brands while shopping from Sainsbury?

a) Strongly Agree

b) Agree

c) Neutral

d) Disagree

e) Strongly Agree

7. Fashionable styles are at your high priority when you go for purchasing clothes?

a) Strongly Agree

b) Agree

c) Neutral

d) Disagree

e) Strongly Agree

8. What is frequency of your visits to restaurants?

e) Very High

f) High

g) Moderate

h) Low

i) Very Low

9. **Which of the following is your preference for spending leisure time?**
a) Theatre and concerts
b) Sports
c) Visiting friends
d) Others

10. **From where do you get information about products and services of Sainsbury?**
a) Newspapers
b) Magazines
c) Television
d) Internet

11. **Do you prefer online shopping over physical shopping from Sainsbury?**
a) Strongly Agree
b) Agree
c) Neutral
d) Disagree
e) Strongly Agree

12. **Which of the following financial planning tools are taken up by you?**
a) Investment in insurance
b) Investment in real estate
c) Investment in stock
d) Credit cards
e) Bank loans